THE SCARLET LETTER

by
Nathaniel Hawthorne

Teacher Guide

Written by
Mary Lovejoy Dennis

Note

The Signet Classic paperback edition of the book published by Penguin Books was used to prepare this guide. The page references may differ in the hardcover or other paperback editions.

Please note: Please assess the appropriateness of this book for the age level and maturity of your students prior to reading and discussing it with your class.

ISBN 1-56137-338-9

Copyright infringement is a violation of Federal Law.

© 2000, 2004 by Novel Units, Inc., Bulverde, Texas. All rights reserved. No part of this publication may be reproduced, translated, stored in a retrieval system, or transmitted in any way or by any means (electronic, mechanical, photocopying, recording, or otherwise) without prior written permission from Novel Units, Inc.

Photocopying of student worksheets by a classroom teacher at a non-profit school who has purchased this publication for his/her own class is permissible. Reproduction of any part of this publication for an entire school or for a school system, by for-profit institutions and tutoring centers, or for commercial sale is strictly prohibited.

Novel Units is a registered trademark of Novel Units, Inc.

Printed in the United States of America.

To order, contact your local school supply store, or—

Novel Units, Inc.
P.O. Box 97
Bulverde, TX 78163-0097

Web site: www.educyberstor.com

Table of Contents

About the Author

Nathaniel Hawthorne was born July 4, 1804, in Salem, Massachusetts, the son of a sea captain who died when Nathaniel was only four. His mother soon moved the family to the Maine woods, where young Nathaniel enjoyed all the pleasures of being a boy in the country. Although he was a reluctant student, he graduated from Bowdoin College in 1825, adding the "w" to his last name at that time. He lived with his mother for the next twelve years, back in Salem, refining his writing skills and seeking an interested publisher.

His first book was self-published. When he realized it was doomed to failure, he recalled as many books as possible and destroyed them. He had been unable to interest a publisher in his many tales and sketches, which he hoped could be published as a collection. Instead, many of his stories appeared in newspapers and magazines, with no credit given to him. Although he began to attain a literary name for himself in 1837 with *Twice-Told Tales,* he was not able to make a living from his writing. He worked at the Custom House in Boston, but resigned after several years to join the Brook Farm Community, an early experiment in communal farming and simple living. Farm work proved harder than he expected, and he had little time for writing. He decided to move to Concord, and married Sophia Peabody, to whom he had been secretly engaged but reluctant to marry due to his financial instability. Thoreau and Emerson were their neighbors in Concord.

At this time, Hawthorne was appointed "Surveyor for the Port of Salem." While working at the Custom House there, he obtained some of the material later presented in "The Custom House," the introductory essay to *The Scarlet Letter.* When the Whigs won the 1848 election, Hawthorne, a Democrat, had to leave his position. In the seven months that followed, he wrote *The Scarlet Letter,* which sold well.

The Hawthornes moved to Lennox, where they became acquainted with Herman Melville. Melville was in the process of writing *Moby Dick,* which he later dedicated to Hawthorne. In the next few years, Hawthorne wrote *The House of the Seven Gables, The Blithedale Romance,* and *A Wonder Book for Girls and Boys.*

In May of 1852, the Hawthornes were finally able to purchase a home of their own in Concord, along with nine acres of land. Here Hawthorne produced *Tanglewood Tales* and *A Life of Pierce.* The latter was written as a campaign piece for Hawthorne's old college friend, Franklin Pierce. When Pierce was elected President, he repaid the favor by appointing Hawthorne United States Consul in England. In 1858, at the end of Pierce's term, Hawthorne and his family spent a year in Italy, where Hawthorne gathered material for *The Marble Faun,* which he wrote the following year in England.

Back at their home in Concord, it seemed that life might finally settle to a pleasant routine for the Hawthornes—but it was not to be. Hawthorne's health began to decline, and in 1864 he died in his sleep. Although he did not enjoy a legendary reputation during his lifetime, today he is considered one of the greatest of classic American writers.

Historical Background

An understanding of the historical context of *The Scarlet Letter* is absolutely essential to comprehension of the text and its themes. A class discussion of why settlers came to America and what these people were like is in order. The first permanent settlement at Jamestown was motivated by economics. Settlers were encouraged to come to America by the Virginia Company, which hoped to benefit in turn through trade with England. Although British mercantilism got a slow start due to disease, famine, and uncooperative Indians, Jamestown and other southern settlements eventually evolved into the antebellum South of plantations, slavery, and wealth. Although there were a few educated aristocrats in the South of the 1600s, most of its residents were illiterate frontiersmen, farmers, and slaves.

In New England things were different. A considerable number of those who settled at Plymouth, Salem, and Massachusetts Bay Colony were learned people, especially the Puritan clergymen. English Puritans were members of the Church of England who advocated reform, in particular less control by the bishop. In 1633, the Church of England came under the control of Archbishop Laud, who vowed to root out these dissenters. The more radical Puritans, followers of John Calvin, fled England to settle in America. They called it "the New Jerusalem." Calvin and his followers put special emphasis on the doctrine of original sin, which maintained that there was really nothing humans could do to mitigate their natural depravity, and that they could only be saved by the grace of God. Also important were the doctrines of providence and predestination, the belief that an omnipotent God decided everything ahead of time. These beliefs compelled them to live by a strict code of ethics found in the literal interpretation of the Bible.

As is the case with most philosophical movements, there were those who were overly zealous. These were the Puritans who burned witches and became hysterical over small transgressions. The Puritans' contribution to American society has been perhaps underrated, for they initiated the town-meeting form of government, popular elections, and common schools. They claim the first college (Harvard) and the first printing press in the colonies, and they produced the most memorable literature before 1740.

Students should realize that Hawthorne was <u>not</u> a Puritan—he wrote his novels in the 19th century, two hundred years after his ancestors arrived in Salem. In the introductory essay to *The Scarlet Letter,* he acknowledges his "ancestral guilt" as a descendent of one of the judges in the Salem witchcraft trials of the late 1600s: "I, the present writer, as their representative, hereby take shame upon myself for their sakes, and pray that any curse incurred by them—as I have heard, and as the dreary and unprosperous condition of the race, for many a long year back, would argue to exist—may be now and henceforth removed."

The Scarlet Letter: **Plot Summary**

The Scarlet Letter takes place in the mid-1600s. It opens with a scene in the village square. A young woman holding a baby is being led from the prison. She is Hester Prynne, and she has been found guilty of adultery. She came to Boston several years before, but her husband never followed and is presumed dead. Hester has been ordered to wear a scarlet letter "A" on the bodice of her dress forever, and today she must stand on the public scaffold for three hours while the townspeople make cruel remarks.

As Hester gazes out over the crowd, she recognizes a misshapen old man—her husband—standing at the edge of the crowd with an Indian. He is a stranger to the townspeople, and inquires about Hester. When he learns of her crime and is told that she refuses to identify the baby's father, he vows that Hester's "partner in sin" will also be punished.

When Hester is taken back to the prison, she is in such a nervous state that the jailer fears for the child. It so happens that the misshapen stranger, who calls himself Roger Chillingworth, is lodging at the jail. The jailer learns that, in addition to being a scientist, Chillingworth has been a captive of the Indians, and has learned about medicinal plants from them. He is called to tend Hester and the baby.

Although Hester fears his wrath, Chillingworth tells her that he blames himself for expecting a beautiful young woman like Hester to be happy in a marriage to him. His anger seems to be directed at the unknown father of the child, but Hester refuses to reveal his name. She does agree, however, not to reveal Chillingworth's true identity, understanding his embarrassment at having an adulterous wife.

When Hester leaves prison, she moves into a small cottage at the edge of town. Her extraordinary needlework skills earn her a living, although she is reviled by those she serves. Hester's own clothing is plain and somber, but Pearl is always dressed elaborately. As Pearl gets older, it becomes apparent that she is rather strange. Although she is very intelligent, she is unruly and refuses to mind her mother. Members of the community say she is the offspring of a demon, and it is only through Reverend Dimmesdale's intervention that Hester is allowed to keep her child.

Reverend Dimmesdale is highly regarded by the townspeople, and they are distressed to realize that his health is failing. The physician, Chillingworth, soon arranges to take up residence in the same house as Dimmesdale. Chillingworth deduces that Dimmesdale's failing health may stem from some unconfessed guilt. After some psychological prying, he becomes convinced that Dimmesdale is Pearl's father.

Late one night, the conscience-tormented Dimmesdale stands on the scaffold as Hester once did. Hester and Pearl, returning from a watch at a deathbed, join him on the scaffold. Dimmesdale is horrified when a flying meteor forms the red letter "A" in the sky, and even more appalled when little Pearl points to Chillingworth, who has been watching them.

Hester decides she must tell Dimmesdale that Chillingworth is her husband, but she first meets with Chillingworth. She tells him that his obsession with punishing Dimmesdale is not only killing the minister, but turning Chillingworth into a fiend. When Hester meets with Dimmesdale in the forest and reveals the secret, he agrees to secretly sail to England with Hester and Pearl to start a new life. The relief and renewed energy he feels make him wonder if he has sold his soul to the devil.

On Election Day, Dimmesdale gives an inspired speech. Hester has quietly booked passage on a ship, but she learns from the captain that Roger Chillingworth plans to sail with them. As Dimmesdale passes through the crowd, not acknowledging Hester or Pearl with so much as a glance, Hester realizes their relationship may not work out. It hardly matters, for soon Dimmesdale is standing on the scaffold confessing that he is Pearl's father. He tears his shirt open to reveal the letter "A," which looks as if it has been burned into his flesh. He then collapses and dies on the platform.

Hester leaves Boston, and Chillingworth dies, willing a fortune to Pearl. Many years later, Hester returns to Boston and becomes a woman whom others seek out for advice and comfort. At her death, she is buried next to Dimmesdale. One tombstone marks both graves.

Note: The introductory essay, "The Custom House," is not included in this synopsis as it is not an integral part of the story. "The Custom House" is autobiographical. It gives lengthy descriptions of the aging and indolent government officials who worked at the Custom House under Hawthorne, the Surveyor. The essay also provides the reader with the "source" for the novel in the form of an old embroidered letter "A" and an explanation written by a former Surveyor. The essay also shows how Hawthorne related to his contemporaries and is a good example of his ability to write satirically.

Prereading Activities

1. Provide students with historical background. Use the information on page 4, but also ask for input from the students. You might use an Attribute Web (see page 17) on the chalkboard using "typical Puritan" as your character, or simply brainstorm the word "Puritan."

2. Provide students with the background information on Hawthorne's life. You might want to point out that, although Hawthorne is considered to be one of the greatest American writers, he was scarcely able to make a living with his craft.

3. Complete the "Anticipation Guide" in the Novel Units® Student Packet. Discuss students' answers in small groups or pairs.

4. Before beginning to read, have students create their own Active Reading Charts, following the diagram below. Explain that after each reading session, the students should take a few minutes to complete the chart for that particular reading section. The completed Active Reading Chart is a useful review tool. It can be checked periodically to assure that students are not lagging behind in comprehension.

Active Reading Chart

What characters have we met so far?	What seems to be the main conflict or problem at this point?	Questions for which I would like to find answers:	My predictions about what will happen next:
Chapters 1-3: *Hester Prynne, her illegitimate child, & Dimmesdale* **Chapters 4-6:**	*Hester is condemned to wear the letter "A" and won't name the baby's father*	*Who is the baby's father? What will Hester's husband do?*	*Hester's husband will come to see her in prison.*

Vocabulary • Discussion Questions
Writing Ideas • Activities

The Custom House

Vocabulary

venerable 18	voluminous 19	besom 19	emoluments 19
progenitor 20	tempestuous 22	indolent 23	vicissitude 23
nonentity 28	evanescent 32	polemical 32	esoteric 34

Note: This introductory essay was added to the beginning of the novel after it was completed. It is not an integral part of the story, and since it is long on description and short on "action," you may elect to have students begin with Chapter One.

Questions for Discussion:
1. In what way is "The Custom House" autobiographical? (Hawthorne was Surveyor at the Salem Custom House. His ancestors were staid government officials who persecuted "witches." He had spent time at Brook Farm.)
2. How does Hawthorne think his ancestors would feel about him? (that he is a worthless failure)
3. Describe the officials who served under Hawthorne. (They were old and lazy. When they did accomplish some small task, they made a great fuss over it.)
4. What traits distinguished the Collector? (He seemed not to think or feel, but acted on instinct. He took great pleasure in food. Although he was almost a nonentity, he was very content.)
5. With what famous writer-philosophers was Hawthorne acquainted? (Emerson, Thoreau, Longfellow)
6. What did Hawthorne find among the old records? (an embroidered scarlet "A" and an explanation written by a former Surveyor named Jonathan Pue)
7. In what way was it fortunate that Hawthorne lost his job? (He had the idea for Hester Prynne's story, and now he had time to write it.)

Critical Thinking for Writing and Discussion:
8. How are some government officials today like the ones Hawthorne describes?
9. How might it be a good thing to lose *your* job?

Chapters 1-3

Vocabulary

sepulchre 55	Utopia 55	edifice 55	physiognomy 57
heterodox 57	infamy 58	autumnal 59	ignominy 61
deportment 62	countenance 64	phantasmagoric 65	visage 67
iniquity 68	tremulous 72		

Questions for Discussion:
1. What is the purpose of chapter 1? (It sets the scene and the mood of the novel.)
2. What sort of story will this be? (a "tale of human frailty and sorrow")
3. What does the rosebush symbolize? ("some sweet moral blossom," i.e., the theme or moral of the story)
4. For what sin is Hester Prynne being punished? How? (For the sin of adultery, she must wear the red letter A on her breast, and she must be subjected to public ridicule for three hours on the scaffold.)
5. Who is with Hester? (her infant daughter, Pearl)
6. How did the Puritan women act? (They were stern and sanctimonious, and some felt Hester deserved to be executed.)
7. What is Mr. Dimmesdale's attitude toward Hester? (He is more sympathetic toward Hester and asks her to name the father of the baby so he too can begin to repent.)
8. Who does Hester recognize in the crowd? Where has he been until now? (her husband; living with the Indians as a captive)
9. What vow does "the stranger" make? (to find out the name of the baby's father)

Critical Thinking for Writing and Discussion:
10. What "bitter but wholesome cup" does Dimmesdale say Hester is denying her partner in sin? (The revelation of his name would mean he could begin to make amends. Now he must live with his guilt.)

Activities:
- Most students today know someone who has had a baby out of wedlock. Through discussion, make the distinction between this situation and adultery. (Hester Prynne was married, but her husband could not be the baby's father because he had been gone for two years.)
- Have the students write answers, with explanations, to the following questions: Do you think it is a *sin* to have a child out of wedlock? Is it a *crime*? Is adultery a sin, a crime, or neither?

- After you have read their answers, discuss the difference in present-day society, between "sin" and "crime." The important thing is to show the students that "sin" implies value judgement, while "crime" is defined by the legal system and even broken down into felonies and misdemeanors. In Puritan society, there was no real distinction between sin and crime, and the church was so much a part of the community that it was its task to judge and punish.

Chapters 4-6

Vocabulary

sagamores 76	peremptory 76	paramour 80	vivify 83
ascetic 86	penitence 87	reviled 88	exhortation 88
contumacious 90	amenable 93	caprice 94	anathema 96

Questions for Discussion:
1. Who did the jailer summon to help little Pearl? Why? (Roger Chillingworth. He was a scientist and herbalist, so was considered a physician. Hester was in a frenzied nervous state due to seeing him in the crowd, and Pearl was suffering from her mother's mood.)
2. Why is Hester afraid to drink what Chillingworth gives her? (She fears he may be trying to poison her out of revenge.)
3. What apology does Chillingworth make? (He blames himself for expecting her to love him.)
4. What vow does Chillingworth make? (to find the baby's father and exact revenge)
5. What does Chillingworth ask Hester to promise? Why? (He asks her not to reveal him as her husband because he would be embarrassed and dishonored if people knew he was the husband of a faithless wife.)
6. When Hester left prison, what did she have to look forward to? (She would be a symbol of sinful passion.)
7. Why didn't Hester simply leave town and pretend to be a widow with a child? (She felt compelled to stay where her sin took place and try to purge her soul.)
8. Where did Hester live? (in a cottage at the edge of town, by the sea)
9. How did Hester make a living? (doing needlework)
10. How did Hester dress? (in coarse, somber clothing) How did she dress Pearl? (fancifully)
11. How was Hester treated in town? (She was snubbed or reviled by those she helped. Clergymen often made her the subject of their sermons.)

12. What insight did the letter seem to give Hester? (a "sympathetic knowledge" of the hidden sins of those who mistreated her)
13. Why was "Pearl" an appropriate name for the baby? (Hester had paid a great price for her.)
14. What behavior of Pearl's concerned Hester and why? (She was wild and undisciplined. Hester feared her peculiarities stemmed from her own guilt and mental state during her pregnancy.)
15. How was the Puritan society's treatment of Pearl especially unfair? (She was not allowed the company of playmates, and in fact was tormented by other children.)
16. What was the first object of which Pearl became aware? (the scarlet letter)
17. What did some of the townspeople say regarding Pearl's paternity? (that she was a "demon offspring")

Critical Thinking for Writing and Discussion:
18. What kind of people in your school or community are shunned or mistreated? In what ways?
19. Puritan standards for the discipline of children were much more stringent than today's. Make a list of the minimum standards of behavior you would teach your three-year-old child.

Activity: Jonathan Edwards' Resolutions for Young People
Jonathan Edwards was a famous Puritan minister who wrote the following code for young Puritans.

"Being sensible that I am unable to do anything without God's help, I do humbly entreat Him by His grace to enable me to keep these resolutions so far as they are agreeable to His will, for Christ's sake. Remember to read over these resolutions once a week.

Resolved, never to DO, BE or SUFFER any thing in soul or body, less or more, but what tends to the glory of God.

Resolved, never to lose one moment of TIME, but to improve it in the most profitable way I possibly can.

Resolved, to live with all my might while I do live.

Resolved, never to do any thing, which I should be afraid to do if it were the last hour of my life.

Resolved to think much on all occasions of my own dying, and of the common circumstances which attend death.

Resolved, to be endeavoring to find out fit objects of charity and liberality.

Resolved, never to do anything out of revenge.

Resolved, never to suffer the least motions of anger to irrational beings.

Resolved, never to speak evil of any person, except some particular good call for it.

Resolved, to maintain the strictest temperance in eating and drinking.

Resolved, never to do any thing, which if I should see in another, I should count a just occasion to despise him for, or think any way the more meanly of him.

Resolved, to study the Scriptures so steadily, constantly, and frequently, as that I may find, and plainly perceive myself to grow in the knowledge of the same.

Resolved, never to speak any thing that is ridiculous, or matter of laughter on the Lord's day.

Whenever I hear anything spoken in conversation of any person, if I think it would be praiseworthy in me, resolved to endeavor to emulate it.

Resolved, after afflictions, to inquire, what I am the better for them; what good I have got and what I might have got by them."

- Share these resolutions with the students. Have each student choose one of the resolutions which they would like to try to pay special attention to over the next week. Also have them choose one which they think is foolish.
- At the end of the week, students should report on their progress in keeping the resolution they chose and also explain if they still find little use for the resolution they chose as foolish. This can be done as a written exercise or in small groups or pairs.
- As an alternate activity, have the students read and discuss Edwards' resolutions and then work in groups to write their own Resolutions for Young People.

Chapters 7-9

Vocabulary

ludicrous 101	intrinsic 102	imperious 102	dauntless 103
cabalistic 104	leech 105	panoply 106	eldritch 107
expatiating 108	mountebank 114	vindicate 117	chirurgical 118
importunate 120	sagacity 123	diabolical 126	

Questions for Discussion

1. What reasons did some of the townspeople have for wanting to take Pearl from Hester? (If Pearl was a "demon child," it was bad for Hester's soul. If Pearl was not a demon child, it was bad for Pearl to be exposed to Hester.)
2. How did Pearl's appearance shock people on the day she and her mother went to visit the governor? (She was dressed in a red velvet tunic with gold embroidery, and looked like a live version of the scarlet letter.)

3. How did Pearl deal with the Puritan children who made fun of them? (She rushed at them, screaming and shouting.)
4. Does Governor Bellingham's house seem to be in keeping with Puritan simplicity? (No, it is very elaborate.)
5. On page 106, use context to define the following: cuirass, gorget, greaves, and gauntlets. (All are parts of a suit of armor.)
6. What was rather bizarre about the armor? (Its convex shape enlarged the reflection of the letter "A" so that Hester seemed to be hiding behind it.)
7. What men do Hester and Pearl meet at the Governor's? (Governor Bellingham, Reverend Wilson, Reverend Dimmesdale, and Roger Chillingworth)
8. What convinces the governor and Reverend Wilson that Pearl should be taken from Hester? (When she is asked, "Who made thee?" Pearl replies that she was plucked from a rosebush by the prison.)
9. What does Hester tell the men? (that she will die before she gives up Pearl)
10. Who speaks in Hester's behalf? (Dimmesdale)
11. How do Pearl and Dimmesdale react to one another? (Pearl takes his hand. He kisses her forehead.)
12. Why was Roger Chillingworth a valuable addition to the town? (His skill in medicine was a rarity.)
13. What is happening to Dimmesdale at this point? (His health is failing.)
14. Rather than a physical ailment, what did Chillingworth decide was the source of Dimmesdale's problems? (an undisclosed guilt)
15. What did some of the townspeople believe about Chillingworth? (that he was Satan's emissary, sent to test Dimmesdale)

Critical Thinking for Writing and Discussion:
16. How are decisions about child custody made today as compared to the 1600s?
17. Who do you think Pearl's father is? Why?

Research Activity: Although Hawthorne gives us an excellent picture of how Puritans regarded sin, he does not include much in the way of description of everyday life in the town. Spend a few class periods at the library to allow students to find out more about Puritan life. A good way to do this is by dividing them into groups, and assigning a separate area of research to each group. Suggested divisions are:
1. History of the Massachusetts Bay Colony
2. What kinds of houses the Puritans built
3. How Puritans made their livings
4. The role of women
5. Food the Puritans ate
6. Clothing the Puritans wore

Chapters 10-12

Vocabulary

askance 129	eccentricities 132	palliate 134	somniferous 135
vestment 135	etherealized 138	imbued 139	infirmity 139
impalpable 142	somnambulism 143	inextricable 144	expiation 144
decorous 147	impute 151	malevolence 151	erudite 152

Questions for Discussion

1. Summarize the conversation between Chillingworth and Dimmesdale about "secret sins." (Chillingworth remarks that he can't understand why some men would rather hide their sins than confess them. Dimmesdale tells him that if certain people were revealed to the world as sinful, they could no longer do God's work.)
2. How has Chillingworth's original wish to see justice done changed? (It has now become an obsession.)
3. What is Chillingworth's explanation to Dimmesdale about his illness? (that it is caused by a spiritual rather than a physical problem) What is Dimmesdale's reaction? (He is offended and upset and runs from the room, delighting Chillingworth.)
4. What do you think Chillingworth saw when he looked under the sleeping Dimmesdale's shirt? (student opinion)
5. How is Dimmesdale now at the mercy of Chillingworth? (Chillingworth can play upon his nerves with little allusions here and there that can be taken two ways. Dimmesdale has actually developed a horror of Chillingworth.)
6. How does Dimmesdale's suffering make him more popular with his congregation? (He is more able to sympathize with other sinners, and this sympathy shows in his sermons. When he professes his own sinfulness, they see it as proof that he is holy.)
7. How does Dimmesdale punish himself for his sin? (whipping himself, fasting, keeping vigils)
8. Where does Dimmesdale go one night? (to stand on the scaffold)
9. Who joins him? (Hester and Pearl)
10. What appears in the sky? (A meteor lights up the sky, and Dimmesdale is sure he sees a huge red letter "A.")
11. Who has been watching them? (Chillingworth)

Critical Thinking for Writing and Discussion:

12. Do you agree with Chillingworth that it is best not to keep guilty secrets?
13. Using a T-chart, compare your first impressions of Dimmesdale with the impressions you now have of him.

Using Character Webs

Attribute webs are simply a visual representation of a character from the novel. They provide a systematic way for the students to organize and recap the information they have about a particular character. Attribute webs may be used after reading the novel to recapitulate information about a particular character or completed gradually as information unfolds, done individually, or finished as a group project.

One type of character attribute web uses these divisions:

- What a character DOES.

   Characters act differently at various times, so have the students think about what the character does in his or her daily life as well as in reaction to the events of the story. For instance, Hester does needlework, gives to the poor, but cries when Pearl is difficult.
- How a character LOOKS.
   It may be helpful for students to close their eyes for a few minutes and visualize the character as they see him or her. Pearl is described as elf-like and so active that she seems to dance on the air. She has dark curly hair, and is usually dressed elaborately.
- How a character FEELS.
   Characters' feelings change. Students should indicate <u>when</u> a character feels a certain emotion. Hester feels shame when she is shunned by the townspeople, fear when Pearl acts like a "demon child," and pride in her work.
- What a character SAYS.
   A character's statements are often the best clues a novelist gives about the person. Chillingworth says things that psychologically torment Dimmesdale. Pearl screams in incoherent anger at children who throw pebbles at her and Hester.

In group discussion about the completed attribute webs for specific characters, you can ask for backup proof from the novel. You can also include inferential thinking. Attribute webs need not be confined to characters. They may also be used to organize information about a concept, object or place.

15

Character Attribute Web

The attribute web below is designed to help you gather clues the author provides about what a character is like. Fill in the blanks with words and phrases which tell what the character does and feels, as well as what the character says and what he or she looks like.

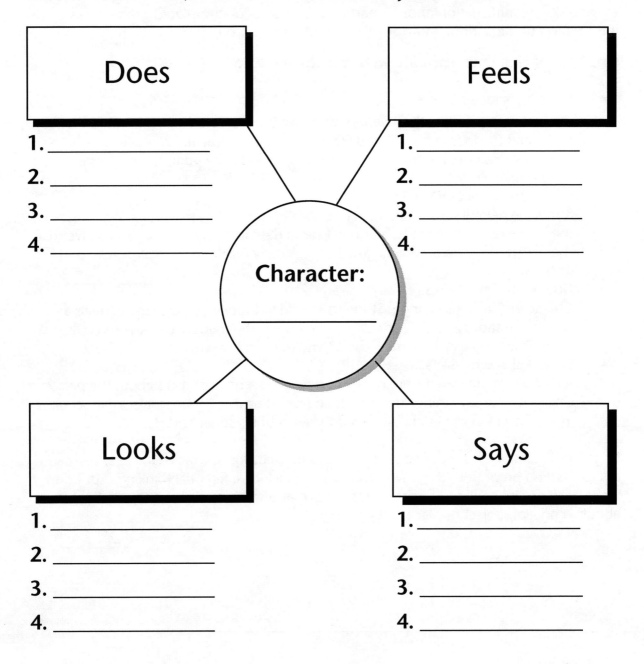

Does

1. _____
2. _____
3. _____
4. _____

Feels

1. _____
2. _____
3. _____
4. _____

Character:

_____

Looks

1. _____
2. _____
3. _____
4. _____

Says

1. _____
2. _____
3. _____
4. _____

Attribute Web

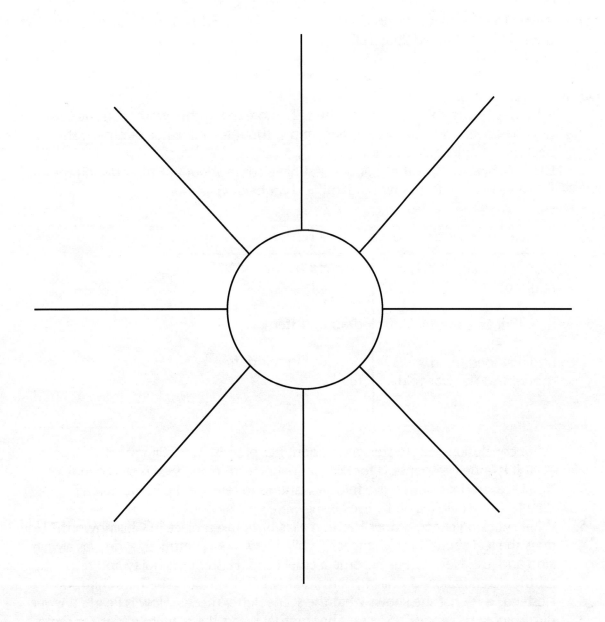

Chapters 13-15

Vocabulary

abased 154	pristine 154	despots 156	propensity 157
speculation 159	stigmatized 159	obviated 160	acquiescing 161
retribution 167	sedulous 168	deleterious 168	nuptial 169
petulant 172	asperity 174		

Questions for Discussion

1. Why was Hester able to "think for herself" more than other women in the town? (She had been cast out by everyone, and without the influence of others, she had become an independent thinker.)

2. Use a T-chart to show the changes that have come about in Hester during the seven years since Pearl's birth. (Sample chart below.)

Hester seven years ago	Hester now
scorned by all—"A" is for adultery	scorned by few—"A" is for "able"
beautiful & warm-looking	drab and stern
undeveloped mind: thought as she was told	developing mind: free thinker

3. What conclusion does Hester reach about her promise to Chillingworth? (that it is largely responsible for Dimmesdale's torture and weakening condition)

4. What reason does Hester give for not wanting to remove the scarlet letter? (She feels it would fall off by itself if she were worthy of its removal.)

5. What shocking changes does Hester realize have taken place in Chillingworth? How does she feel about these changes? (While he was never attractive, he was always kind and just. Now he has become a cruel fiend. Hester feels guilty and responsible for the deterioration of Chillingworth, but "be it sin or no," she hates him.)

6. Hester asks Pearl if she knows what the scarlet letter means. How is Pearl's answer disturbingly perceptive? (She says her mother wears the scarlet "A" for the same reason Dimmesdale holds his hand over his heart.)

7. In view of Pearl's precocity, what does Hester consider doing? (explaining the real significance of the letter to her)
8. What does Hester finally tell Pearl is her reason for wearing the letter? (for the sake of the gold thread)

Critical Thinking for Writing and Discussion:
9. Reread Chillingworth's closing speech at the end of Chapter 14. What is he really telling Hester? What do his religious beliefs seem to be?
10. Do you think Hester made a wise decision in not telling Pearl the truth about the scarlet letter at this point? Would she have understood? At what age should she be told, if not now?

Activity: Hawthorne's Symbolism

Symbolism is the use of an object, character, or event to represent something else. *The Scarlet Letter* is often regarded as the first novel to be published in the United States that used symbolism. The letter "A" itself maybe the first symbol students will think of. While it literally stands for the sin of adultery, to Hester it also symbolized a lifetime of humiliation. As Hester proves she is trying hard to purge herself of sin, people begin to say that the letter stands for "Able." The "A" reminds Dimmesdale of his own guilt; he even sees it emblazoned in the sky—although the townspeople believe this particular "A" stands for "Angel," because Governor Winthrop has just ascended into heaven.

A discussion of the symbolism of the letter "A" should get the students interested in finding some of the other symbols in the novel. Some symbols are listed below followed by the meanings upon which critics generally agree.

> **the scaffold:** acknowledgement of sin before the public
> **the forest:** a free, wild place where the Puritan code does not apply, but also a place of evil and darkness
> **Reverend Wilson:** the Church
> **Governor Bellingham:** the State
> **Mistress Hibbins:** Satan; witchcraft
> **the color black:** evil
> **iron:** strength, whether Puritan code or Satan's power
> **sunshine and light:** truth, redemption

The main characters are all symbols that relate to sin. **Hester** is sin confessed and repented. **Dimmesdale** is the guilt of unconfessed sin. **Chillingworth** is self-destructive revenge for sin. **Pearl** is the innocent result of sin, and also a living reminder of it.

Chapters 16-18

Vocabulary

scrofula 176	loquacity 178	atheist 182	Pentecost 182
contiguity 183	malignity 184	trammelled 190	subjugated 193
denizens 194	choleric 194		

Questions for Discussion

1. Why do Pearl and Hester walk into the forest? (Hester hopes to meet Dimmesdale as he is returning home, and tell him about Chillingworth.)
2. What does the sunshine symbolize? (Pearl says it is running away from Hester because of the letter "A." The light—and redemption—cannot be Hester's.)
3. To what does Hawthorne compare the forest walk? (Hester's wanderings in a "moral wilderness.")
4. What stories has Pearl heard about the Black Man? To whom is she referring? (She has heard that the Black Man, or Satan, haunts the forest, gets people to join him by signing his book, and then puts his mark on them. She has heard that the "A" is his mark on Hester. Hester tells her that is true—she met the Black Man once.)
5. What does the brook symbolize? (sorrow)
6. How does Dimmesdale look when Hester sees him approaching? (He is haggard and feeble-looking.)
7. What does Dimmesdale say about penance and penitence? (that he has had plenty of penance but no penitence) What does he mean? (Although he has tried to atone for his sin through his good works, he has still not confessed his guilt, so there can be no real atonement.)
8. What is Dimmesdale's reaction to the news about Chillingworth? (He cries out in actual pain, clutches his heart, and says he cannot forgive Hester for letting the torture by Chillingworth take place for so long.)
9. What does Dimmesdale say is Chillingworth's sin? (He "violated the sanctity of a human heart.")
10. How does Hester become Dimmesdale's strength, and what does she convince him to do? (She tells him he must not lie down and die, and that they can leave Boston and start a new life together with their daughter.)
11. Once the decision is made, how does Dimmesdale feel? (He feels a great relief and sense of joy. For the first time in years, there seems to be hope for the future.)
12. How does Hester change when the decision is made? (She removes the scarlet letter, lets her hair fall around her shoulders, and seems beautiful again.)

13. How does the forest itself change once the decision is made? (The gloom changes to sunshine and light. The brook now has a "merry gleam.")
14. Why does the scene between Hester and Dimmesdale seem different than any other in the book so far? (This is a "love scene." There is relief and joy rather than loneliness and despair. They have nothing to hide from one another.)
15. Why is it important to Hester that Pearl have a father? (She hopes Dimmesdale will be able to help her figure out the strange little girl.)

Critical Thinking for Writing and Discussion:
16. Compare the points of view of society that Hester and Dimmesdale have developed over the past seven years. Why is it so easy for Hester to make the decision to leave Boston, while it is difficult for Dimmesdale?
17. Pearl seems perfectly at home in the forest. Does this make sense?

Activity: "The Trial of Hester Prynne"
Hester Prynne was "lucky" according to many in Boston because she didn't receive the maximum penalty for her sin—death by hanging. In the following activity, students become the characters in the novel and Hester Prynne is called for a re-trial.

Students should work in two groups. One group presents a re-trial in 17th-century Boston. The other group will present a retrial in modern times. They will need to spend several days preparing for the new trials. The following characters should be represented:

Group One: 17th-century Boston

Hester Prynne, who is accused of adultery
The Prosecuting Attorney, who is a direct representative of the church
Ex-governor John Winthrop, who maybe called to testify
Governor Bellingham, the governor of Massachusetts
Reverend Wilson, a staunch leader of the Puritan church
One of Hester's clients for whom she has done needlework
Roger Chillingworth, newly arrived in town (Hester's husband)
Arthur Dimmesdale, the father of Hester's child
Various townspeople who will speak for or against Hester
The judge, who will decide the sentence based on what the others say

Group Two: Modern Times Retrial

Hester Prynne, who is accused of adultery
The Defense Attorney, who will try to prove Hester's innocence
The Prosecuting Attorney, who will try to prove Hester's guilt
The great, great grandson of governor John Winthrop, who may be called to testify
The current governor of Massachusetts
Reverend Wilson, a staunch leader of a church
One of Hester's clients for whom she has done needlework
Roger Chillingworth, newly arrived in town (Hester's husband)
Arthur Dimmesdale, the father of Hester's child.
Various townspeople who will speak for or against Hester
The judge, who will decide the sentence based on what the others say

THE JURORS: Group One will serve as Group Two's jurors. Group Two will serve as Group One's jurors.

Procedure:

1. The teacher should open the court hearing and swear in the jurors.
2. The Prosecutor makes an opening statement, introducing the nature of the case, giving a summary of the facts, and stating the charges.
3. Defense: In the 17th-century trial, Hester must speak for herself. In the modern trial, the defense attorney should make an opening statement denying the charges.
4. The Prosecutor calls and examines witnesses. The questions should be determined in advance, and the students playing the parts of witnesses should have prepared answers.
5. The defense (Hester or the defense attorney) should also have a chance to call witnesses.
6. Each side should present closing arguments.
7. The jurors should confer and announce their decision.
8. The judge pronounces the sentence.

Chapters 19-21

Vocabulary

mollified 198	multitudinous 201	irrefragable 203	obeisance 205
impiety 206	archfiend 207	buckramed 208	potentate 208
purport 209	plebeian 212	preternaturally 213	mien 213
festal 216	jocularity 217	depredations 219	
animadversion 219	galliard 219		

Questions for Discussion

1. What is there about Pearl that has caused Dimmesdale "many an alarm"? (the resemblance between him and the child)
2. What was the cause of the estrangement between Pearl and Hester? (Hester's intimate conversation with Dimmesdale had made Pearl feel left out and a little jealous. In addition, her mother now looked different without her scarlet letter, and with her hair down.)
3. What must Hester do to placate Pearl? (put the scarlet letter back on)
4. Hester is willing to put the scarlet letter, her acknowledgement of sin, back on, and Pearl readily kisses her. Pearl is not so receptive to the kiss of Dimmesdale. What does she ask him that may explain why? (Pearl asks if he will go back into the town, hand in hand with them, and Hester must tell her that he will not.)
5. What specific plans have Hester and Dimmesdale made? (to return to England on a ship that departs in four days)
6. How did Dimmesdale feel when he returned to town? (full of energy)
7. What disturbing things did Dimmesdale feel like doing? (making some blasphemous suggestions regarding the communion supper when talking to one of the church deacons; telling the eldest female church member that the soul is not immortal; saying something lecherous to one of the church's young women; teaching some little children some bad words; telling dirty jokes with a sailor)
8. What did his wicked impulses make Dimmesdale fear? (that he had sold himself to the devil)
9. Who knew about Dimmesdale being in the forest? (Mistress Hibbins)
10. Of what "sin" is Dimmesdale now guilty? (He has yielded to deliberate choice.)
11. What is Dimmesdale's attitude when he sees Chillingworth? (Dimmesdale tells him he'll have no more need of his medicine.)
12. What would Hester have liked to say to the crowd in the market place? ("Look your last on the scarlet letter!")

13. What does Pearl ask about Reverend Dimmesdale? (if he will hold out his hands to them) What is she told? (that she mustn't greet him)
14. What gave the Election Day crowd some diversity? (There were Indians and sailors.)
15. What disturbing news did the commander of the ship give Hester? (that Chillingworth had also booked passage on the ship)

Critical Thinking for Writing and Discussion:
16. What does Hawthorne's description of holidays in England provide? Why do you think he included it at this point in the novel?
17. What do you think Dimmesdale's refusal to publicly acknowledge Hester and Pearl says about his character?

Activity: The Genre of *The Scarlet Letter*
Hawthorne called *The Scarlet Letter* a romance. Review the following list of the elements of Romanticism, and discuss whether *The Scarlet Letter* possesses them.

- love of nature as the revelation of Truth
- sympathetic interest in the past
- interest in the psychology of emotions
- criticism of the norm
- mysticism
- the individual as the center of literature

Chapters 22-24

Vocabulary

comprised 221	clarion 221	morions 222	necromancy 225
indefatigable 228	disquietude 228	pathos 232	apotheosized 233
lurid 237	escutcheon 245	gules 245	

Questions for Discussion
1. How does Hester feel as Dimmesdale passes by? (She is disappointed that he doesn't even glance her way, and wonders if there can really be a future for them.)
2. What does Mistress Hibbins say about Dimmesdale? (that he has "met the Black Man" and that his sins will be revealed)

3. What is ironic about the scene in the square as Dimmesdale gives the Election Day speech? (Dimmesdale, giving an eloquent speech, is being admired by the townspeople while Hester, who he will soon join, is an object of curiosity to those who have never seen her before. She is the source of his strength, yet this goes totally unacknowledged.)
4. What is Dimmesdale finally driven to do? (to confess his guilt in front of everyone)
5. In what way does Dimmesdale's action defeat Chillingworth? (Chillingworth's power over Dimmesdale was that he knew his secret. Now there is nothing to hide.)
6. Why does Dimmesdale expose his chest? (because there is a mark of sin on it)
7. Summarize Dimmesdale's dying actions and words. (He asks God to forgive Chillingworth, asks Pearl for a kiss, and tells Hester he does not think they will find happiness in eternity together.)
8. How are Pearl's actions especially significant? (When she cries and kisses Dimmesdale, she is conferring a kind of forgiveness on him. All along, she has wanted him to stand with her and her mother. Dimmesdale has finally done the right thing.)
9. What purposes does the final chapter serve? (It contains the moral and lets us know what happened to Hester, Pearl, and Chillingworth.)
10. Hawthorne specifically states the moral of the story. What is it? (page 242—"Be true! Be true! Be true! Show freely to the world, if not your worst, yet some trait whereby the worst may be inferred.") What does this mean?
11. What does Hawthorne say about hatred and love? (that they are so close philosophically that they are "essentially the same")
12. Who, in Hawthorne's view, was guilty of the worst sin? (Chillingworth)
13. What is the "happy ending" in the story? (Hester and Pearl did find a new life. Pearl inherited all Chillingworth's money. Pearl married, and Hester became a grandmother. As the stern Puritan code became more relaxed, Hester returned to her little cottage and became an advisor to other women. At her death, she was buried near Dimmesdale, with one tombstone marking both graves.)

Critical Thinking for Writing and Discussion:
14. What are some of the themes of *The Scarlet Letter*? Is the moral the same as the theme?
15. Do you agree that love and hatred are essentially the same? Explain.

Activity: Story Map
Have the students complete the story map which appears on the following four pages. They should create a new title for each chapter and briefly summarize its events.

Story Map

Review each chapter in the novel. Write a new title that will help you to remember the main events of each chapter. Then write a sentence or two to summarize the chapter's main events.

Original Title   **New Title**

The Prison Door   _____

Summary: _____

_____

The Market Place   _____

Summary: _____

_____

The Recognition   _____

Summary: _____

_____

The Interview   _____

Summary: _____

_____

Hester at Her Needle   _____

Summary: _____

_____

Original Title	New Title
Pearl	_____
Summary: _____	
_____	
The Governor's Hall	_____
Summary: _____	
_____	
The Elf-Child and the Minister	_____
Summary: _____	
_____	
The Leech	_____
Summary: _____	
_____	
The Leech and His Patient	_____
Summary: _____	
_____	
The Interior of a Heart	_____
Summary: _____	
_____	
The Minister's Vigil	_____
Summary: _____	
_____	

	Original Title	**New Title**

Original Title   **New Title**

Another View of Hester

_____

Summary: _____

_____

Hester and the Physician

_____

Summary: _____

_____

Hester and Pearl

_____

Summary: _____

_____

A Forest Walk

_____

Summary: _____

_____

The Pastor and His Parishioner

_____

Summary: _____

_____

A Flood of Sunshine

_____

Summary: _____

_____

Original Title	New Title

The Child at the Brookside

Summary: _____

_____

The Minister in a Maze

Summary: _____

_____

The New England Holiday

Summary: _____

_____

The Procession

Summary: _____

_____

The Revelation of the Scarlet Letter

Summary: _____

_____

Conclusion

Summary: _____

_____

Suggested Essay Topics

1. Define symbolism and show how Hawthorne used it in *The Scarlet Letter*.

2. Summarize the elements of Romantic literature, and explain which of these elements are contained in *The Scarlet Letter*. Be sure to give specific examples.

3. Explain the theme of morality (good vs. evil) in terms of *The Scarlet Letter*. In particular, concentrate on Hester and Dimmesdale. How do they deal with their sins privately and publicly? What is the outcome of their ability (or lack thereof) to cope with the public and private perception of their sins?

4. Discuss the ability of the characters in this novel to forgive. What, who, and why are they able or unable to forgive? What are the results?

5. Discuss how Hawthorne used Pearl as a symbol throughout the novel.

6. Choose another author who was writing at the same time as Hawthorne. Read some of his/her short fiction, and compare the styles of the two writers.

7. There are two primary settings in the novel. Compare and contrast these two settings, and show why they are effective.

8. Choose one of the main characters in *The Scarlet Letter*. Analyze the character in terms of the following: his or her main problem and its resolution; how the character grows or changes; whether or not the reader can really empathize with the character.

9. Choose the five most important scenes in the novel. Summarize each scene, and tell why you feel it is important.

10. Describe Puritan beliefs, and tell how Hawthorne represented them in the novel.

Evaluation: Rubric for Essay-Writing

The following is a suggested set of criteria for grading student essays. It can be altered in any way that fits the specific needs of a class. We encourage you to share the evaluation criteria with your students before they write their essays. You may even want to use this form as a self-grading or partner-grading exercise.

Criterion	Maximum # Points
1. **Focus:** Student writes a clear thesis and includes it in the opening paragraph.	10
2. **Organization:** The final draft reflects the assigned outline; transition words are used to link ideas.	15
3. **Support:** Sufficient details are cited to support the thesis; extraneous details are omitted.	15
4. **Detail:** Each quote or reference is explained (as if the teacher had not read the book); ideas are not redundant.	15
5. **Mechanics:** Spelling, capitalization, usage are correct.	15
6. **Sentence Structure:** The student avoids run-ons and fragments. There is an interesting variety of sentences.	10
7. **Verbs:** All verbs are in the correct tense; sections in which plot is summarized are in the present tense.	10
8. **Total Effect of the Essay:** Clarity, coherence, overall effectiveness.	10

TOTAL_____

Comments:

Notes